The Island Never
Burned So Bright

Jonathan D. Pigno

Copyright © 2014 Jonathan D. Pigno
All rights reserved.

ISBN: 0692264590
ISBN 13: 9780692264591
Library of Congress Control Number: 2014914322
57 Press, Staten Island, NY

*For Mom and Dad, my pulse in the vein of a phrase.
There is no truer grace than the devotion of a parent to a child.
To them, I owe these words.*

*In memory of John D.,
a better man now departed, a hero called too soon.*

I Never Would Have Thought

I was told
You found certain solace
In the sanctuary of cradling words
Rocking us to and fro
Like back-and-forth
Bottles at sea
Reliant on the ebb of tides
Leaving no choice but to drift
Or using as lighted dark
Like moons crescent and near
As the hours that remained elapsed
And the growl of famished organs
Turned deadly
From thirst to need
With screams so silently held
Parched and lacking water
Quieted
By the withdrawn voice
Of your parents then sitting vigil
Alone near wired beds
And the hum of plastic hearts
Keeping the beeps alive
As you sifted through the hands of saints
And fell from the lips of God
As he spoke of ultimate freedom
In the moment when never was now
And the cancer took stars from your eyes
And placed them outside that window
High above doctors and lies
Hospitals or feeble attempts
As the nurses kissed you again
And the word of endings was scripture
Shot like mortars of halos
Gospel

Inscribing the skies
Streaked at the time of your leaving
The crossing from pain to truth
In the absence of explanations.

Yes,
You read my words
Well before you wrote them all
Or altered this voice forever
Because I can't
Ever seem to know.

That's
What I have been told.

It's what
I'd like to believe.

Table of Contents

Dedication · iii
    I Never Would Have Thought · vi

Introduction · xiii

North Site, South Site · 1
    The Letter between These Sheets (One Day) · · · · · · · · · · · · · · 3
    Laundry List · 5
    Trying with Your Gut · 6
    Grief of Waking · 7
    Body of Worth · 9
    Take the Blame · 10
    Oppositional Behavior · 11
    Bodine Creek · 12
    Thinning Branch · 14
    It's Been an Honor · 15
    Dilated Eyes (Capsized) · 17

Victory Boulevard · 19
    Just Off Castleton · 21
    I Read Fante Last Night (Tomb of Ink) · · · · · · · · · · · · · · · · · 23
    Our Garden (Thinking Rationally) · · · · · · · · · · · · · · · · · · · 25
    Wish of a Pen · 26
    Open Book · 27
    Sullen Mathematics · 28
    We Hung Out (War) · 30
    Taking the Initiative · 32
    Beg for Applause · 33
    Saw a Movie · 34
    Button Stuck · 37
    We the Aimless · 39
    Sudden Turns · 44

Carousel (Richmond Avenue) · 47
    Willowbrook (Till Next Time) · 49
    Forever Hold Your Peace · 51
    Never Date a Hippie ('Cause You'll Fall in Love and
    She Won't Stay) · 53
    Sitting Room · 54
    Note on Table · 56
    You Told Me to Watch the Moon · 57
    The Dance after the Ceremony (Nine O'Clock Sharp) · · · · · · · · · 58
    The Glass Cabinet · 59
    Misaligned · 60
    Happy Toys · 61
    Male Gaze · 63
    Postmanic Pixie Syndrome · 65
    Last Time I Need Something to Sleep · 67
    Boarded Up · 70

Sharrotts Road · 73
    Wreck of Prose · 75
    To Live, Love, and Die in Suburbia · 76
    Category Unknown · 78
    Lighthouse · 79
    Tide · 80
    Behind a Good Man · 81
    Why It Hurts · 82
    Gallery · 83
    Blossomed Muse · 84
    Frayed Nerve · 86
    Priorities (Make Them Right) · 87
    Leaps of Faith · 89
    Father Capodanno · 91
    I (Fear) New York · 93
    Prime Mover · 96
    Blockbuster · 98
    Twin Lights · 102

  Run (as Far as You Can) · 105
  Dumb Philosopher · 107
  Carried (from Water) · 108

Acknowledgments · 111

About the Author · 113

Introduction

This is not a story but memories in broken hymns—prayers and unsung legacies as appeals to the injured few. It's a poem of coveted angels and a chronicle of their voice, a lust for the allure of heavens and redemption here and now. It's an ache for the missing daydreams and curse of omitted innocence, valiance turned to fury, and agony in its wake. It's truth in unruly gospel and methods for the raging damned—an image, fault, or vision: a vocation of discontent. It is everything I'd ever valued and sullied in righteous anger, philosophized out of laziness, or idealized in lack of meaning. It's madness, lies, and empathy—the vestige of a perfect girl. It's the paradox of hopeful nihilism and crisis of growing faith. It's religion in crowded places and the suspicion of becoming lost. It's a storm in the eye of tomorrow and sun in the distant past—freedom in flooded basements and childhoods out to sea.

It's a kiss of the living goddess and shadow of the eternal muse. It's what I always hoped to say if she ever just gave me the chance.

It's rubble beneath the surface. It's cracks in invisible walls.
It's the feeling that every moment is ablaze from a hateful sun.
It's bright; it's fire; it's permanent.
It's fantastic. It's real.
It's home.

North Site, South Site

The Letter between These Sheets (One Day)

I refused to write you an elegy because moonlight still gleams in this heart—shimmering across the page like beams on darkened waters, shadowed in dusk and turmoil as the night penetrates written skies, black and elegant cursive surrounding this bed of stars, for which God performed sonatas of galaxies hushed in the gaping distance and captured their fatal poetry in the ink of eternal verse.

I finally admit the delusion of passing my genes in speech. Forgive my twisted perversion of copulating with the abstract phrase. This muse is a twisted element—a building block of chemical nothing, enveloped in the sex of knowing as she breathes life and words on paper.

Anything but love and flesh, everything but the stretch of your arms.

If meeting you was my certainty, then this letter is the broken space—a final decree of loneliness by which the death of feeling is provoked. You are forever my other half, perpetually a stain of blood—my own, my essence, my vein—torn from the rapids of rage out of an empty shell of ruins, now a standard of IVs and operating tables as the radiation bridges distance and death.

The pain will just call me home. The particles now take your place.

The prodding reminds me of you. The smell is a sterile emotion, a vacant hole of compassion with the wiring of a human case.

Unnecessary, but oh-so-fortunate—to be relieved by doctors and scripts, promises and office visits, with daydreams of literary bliss.

Composing a note on my phone and imagining the grace of those greats—looking down from an absent heaven and blessing me with the halo of arguments: Fante, Kerouac, and Selby; Mansfield, Lawrence, and Woolf.

One day I'll be a writer. Yes, one day, this hand will speak.

More than your lies ever could.

More than these empty sheets.

Laundry List

I'm trained in harboring inadequacy. Rattled by irrational fears.
Loathing of belief and science.
Traumatized by weddings and fairy tales.
Assaulted by living phantoms.
Befriended by praying ghosts.
Fixated on tragic endings.
Enamored with painful beginnings.
Flawed in vengeful honesty.
Arrogant in a passing glance.
Judgmental without a platform.
Captivated by solemn elements.
Imprisoned with fleeting smiles.
Jailbroken through lingering frowns.
Liberated on irony's wings.
Discovered through haphazard miracles.
Vindicated in scarlet ink.
Bloodied by the girl of my dreams.
Laid by a demented muse.
Scuffed in fistfights with glory.
Dejected by proper professions.
Taken with horror and honesty.
Debating on a mix of the two.
Muddled between the lines of both.
Slain by the laugh of God.
Resurrected in the embers of faith.
Believing the lie of moments.
Alive and ostracized for the taking.
This fucked-up pen of confessions.
Faulted on words alone.

Trying with Your Gut

I too
Am a loser
Unrefined
Indisposed
Selfish and sinfully brash
Cocked like a smoking barrel
Swagger the inspired aim
Taking shots
In darkened corners
Blindfolds
Covered in arrows
As the boom traces lips
Of silence
And ringing death
Kissing the widening curve
Its ricochet
A firm denial
Subliminal sin and devotion
Victim
Of elegant crimes
A bleeding heart
With holes
To feel the wind accentuate
The pain caught in its angle
A breeze
On blazing trails
To what pleasure
Do I owe this majesty
Of a laughing
Lover's gun?

GRIEF OF WAKING

I am just a man
Deprived of needed sleep
Shackled to raging dawn
Rattled behind tired eyelids
As I seek
This empty verse
Inquisitive and defined
On the linens
Of handcuffed mornings
Locks and missing links
Woven like sullen threads
Tears on the warmth of pillows
Beauty his last resort
Treading this speaking hall
Into darkness
Into memory
Into daylight on tired fingers
Onward
Like ticking labor
Ahead of me
The winding curve
Of clocks and perpetual dogs
With tickets around their throats
Tattoos on crippled arms
Sore like a poor fool's pocket
Maddened like a rich thief's hope
Gazing at the climbing sun
Signaling another day
Just a twisted
Yet fleeting instance
Lost to oddities and endings
Bullshit
For wallets and women
Solace

In perpetual nothing
Regret
Ambition
And sorrow
Wound around your ankles
Pulling you back to bed
Repeating the swollen cycle
Over and over again
Written like the death
Of husbands
Certain as
The hand of God.

Body of Worth

There are authors;
Then there are
Writers—
Idle seekers,
Bullets of angst
Who thirst
For spirits of transience
And live
For the fuck of madness;
Love
For the strain of death
As the liquor
Narrates their traumas,
Stirs the bile of instinct,
And vomits
The fear of meaning
As they face
The last hour
Alone.

Take the Blame

What effort
Does it take
To verbalize
The loss of self
And in feeling
Fake all knowledge
Of the circumstance
Through which I write
Reality
Like a cause
A flame
In the court of stars
On trial
For the sin of embers
Where light
Is a valued fault.

Oppositional Behavior

I made him
A subtle suggestion
To quell
The pervasive nausea
With deliberate
And miscreant acts
That spoke
Of God in our midst
Contrary to idle moments
Speaking
To the fraud of days
And great disillusionment
Of hours
His aggression couldn't dispose
Perhaps then
He would face sobriety
From panic
Or nerves
And needles
Outlined
In the loop of cursive
He wrote
On the cellar door.

Bodine Creek

A bum
Beneath the overpass
Drank splendor
From his bag,
Blew kisses
To stolen cars,
And feared
The local police.

I caught him
Counting curses
Graffitied on mossy pavement
In the span
It took his timepiece
To realize
He was cracked.
From the gears
Of ticking perversity,
He admired like a child
Far from vicious days
Of gazers with empty dreams.

I asked him
What it was like
To be a victim
Under the bridge;
He told me
It was preferable
To gasp for passing life
Instead of
Begging for scraps
From those who have passed before.
I think I knew
What he meant,

Lighting fires
At the edge of the creek
In the night
Of a jealous city
Whose unfortunate
Knew the truth.

His flame
Would keep them warm.

His sleeping bag
Had room for two.

Thinning Branch

How do we
Even breathe
When the torture
Is just to live
And collect
The passing seconds
With daydreams
Padding the walls
Of lunacy in our cells
Ticking
Of clockwork minutes
And efforts
Like heaving lungs
The gears of corrupted will
And breathlessness
Of our happiness
The contentment
Come and gone

No leaf
Ever stays
Stationary
It falls
When
The branch
Grows
Thin.

It's Been an Honor

Salute
To the dying world
That left me
A carcass for scraps
And responsibility
Its pretentious fury
For the suicide
Of permanent kids.

Juveniles
Raised to be poets
Youngsters
Battling artlessness
Too difficult
For the means of idealism
Too easy
To be conquered in trying.

Gather all ye grownups
The fuckers
The bankers
The workmen.

Conjure the fears
Of your wallets
Strive for
A waste of your souls.

Put
All your faith
In the cowardice
Of hiding
Behind walls
Of your fathers

The lust and neglect
Of your mothers
The bitter and just rage
Of your sons.

Let your daughters
Make love
To the prophets
The ones
With the brushes and paints.

The others
With melody and moodiness
The inkwells
Melancholy and brash
And vision
Wrapped in sheets of instinct
As their fluids
Become the blood of the whole.

It's been an honor
To know you
As a bolt
In the deadlock of sin.

It's my pleasure
To perish from sadness
Knowing meaning
Was a game
That was rigged.

Dilated Eyes (Capsized)

My sleep
Is never rest
Coming off
An upturned wave
Living in
A capsized vessel
Burst
At the hull from pressures
As the tide
Still beckons my voyage
In the fog
That has clouded my vision
And dilated
The pulsing blackness
Of my eyes
From harrowing nightfall
Of these winded and salted starboards
And the tilt
Of a bending bow
Embraced by a loving brine
An abyss with flowing omniscience
At the heart of a bleeding ocean
To a man
Forever lost at sea
Known
As a causer of storms.

Victory Boulevard

Just Off Castleton

That's the way
They had to live
But it still could be called
Injustice
How the smell
Of ethnic cooking
Mingled with flying pests
And the carpet
Reeked of apathy
From knowing
The best was last
And all
They could ever afford
Was the disparity's
Beck and call
And the neighborhood lines
Were crafted
As the tough guys
Moved next door
The *nonnas* and Irish grandmas
Feuded on another shore
With a line and crafted prejudice
Ignoring their struggling life
A portion just as meaningful
But bordering a different beach
Where the tankers faced the terrace
And tires lined the streets
The homes weren't built for pleasure
And business was a desperate need
Not excess or petty cash
To buy some imported meats
On Sundays for screaming aunts
Or hold an undue birthday
In the most elaborate halls

This thievery called necessity
And the driving of fancy cars
Attendance of private academies
And behold
The lie of success
When the crossing of a single block
Can change the entire world
The schools
In which we teach
The quality
Of daily life
So different from summer cookouts
Obscured
By the cul-de-sac fence.

I Read Fante Last Night (Tomb of Ink)

And still I cross those ruins as daybreak offers a glimpse of regions bound in mystery and relics within our midst—beyond travels and distant promise, fortunes or failures sold, the labors of mingling journeys and paths intersected of old.

To explore now is to converge—to vanish into singularity, to darken a similar shadow.

This quest is a shaded vengeance; let us kill in light and dark—the charcoal in our fingernails as we capture the dying landscape, illustrate the remaining waste as we contour the lingering spark by the edge of a pointed tip assured of God's demise to dominate the whole of nature and make beauty his bastard child.

It's here in the fields of sympathy, caught in the swell of antics—fallacies of locking vines flourished on sacred ground. Plant life and decaying remnants, abandoned in the spite of sin, now slumbering in quiet agony among the valleys of holy punishment, tropics of scattered angels fallen to spread their news and keep ecstasy a hallowed secret from disciples of plaster hearts. Children of champagne virtue, baptized in glitter and vomit—a gesture of new religion, in clubs, pills, and rituals with witch doctors spinning vinyl.

We all crumble apart in the hands of saints and giants.

We all become a valiant tale in the effort of conquering titans.

Literature isn't a gesture; it's a history of reckless abandon—a chronicle of glorious deadbeats: liars, beggars, and cowards.

I've cried enough hours in yearning to believe in the truth of this pen, to rest my soul on trying with the collected tomes of *now* shining from the weight of its hopes—glistening and liquid ethics, polished and refined in antiquity—so appealing to the ends of their goal, divinity on spoken fragments. The price of a golden phrase is now worth the silent means, indicative of glorious struggle and valued by the passage of days—time the penultimate test, hindsight the critic of ages—ready to vanquish talent with the scrutiny of years to come.

This era is one of nonsense, how writers aren't valued enough—not nearly in the context of gospel that liberates what's left of the stars (conquered as they are by science and hubris of men toasting drinks to the rape of the muse).

I'm tired of bearing these burdens, but I'm willing to tip the scales if it means charting the empty graves of artists obscured by promise and heroes fallen to genius, immortalized in hidden monuments and reflected in breaking stone.

OUR GARDEN (THINKING RATIONALLY)

It's a stake on irony's needle
Being drawn back to sudden tables,
Thrones of momentous tasks,
Corners and shadowed bastions
Overlooking the industrial park
Set against passing highways,
And calls to similar ends,
Where I caught that fleeting gaze
Of thorns and leverage in your eyes,
Vines on the base of your tongue,
Cuttings and stagnant water
Trimmed in the vase of your heart.
Now I'm a part of your garden,
Buried in seed and tomorrows,
Suffocated on yesterday's soil,
Scrounging in dirt for a cause,
When the coffin is a blossom of thought
Left to the ground's devices,
Affirmed in its airless trench,
Gutted in speech and nothingness,
Like monologues of buried men
Sucking on roots of torment
In time spent gardening with you.
Their demise was thinking rationally
And speaking for the girl too soon,
Returning to the grave with flowers
Only to find themselves underfoot.

Wish of a Pen

I'm afraid
I've lost these words
In the pursuit of petty cash
Thievery and wry ambition
Contrary to meaningful dreams
Explicit yet
Undiagnosed
The frailty of a running phrase
Finality of a dying cause
Loose change on an open page
Wanderlust behind closed doors
Severed
Acknowledged
Now deficient
The outpouring of weakness in ink
Tantrums of a failing soul
The meandering of an open book
Seeking its closing term
Punctuation
Or some other gauge
That tells of its potential madness
And illness like delusions in script.

OPEN BOOK

My words
Are an idle vision
Timeless in their waste
A veil of darkened hours
A room with lifted curtains
Resisting the poet's gaze
Refuting a writer's sin
Closed to familiar eyes
But worn as a crown of text
Wedged
Between faith and nothing
To keep this door
Ajar.

Sullen Mathematics

I entertain
These vacuous fears
Because I'm
Lost
In irrational orbit
Spanning
The uncertain black
Careening
On tilted thoughts
Set into
Widening space
An abyss of starry lies
Speckled
With the glimmer of promise
As I round
The brink of creation
And fall
In the gravity of meaning
Your existence
A proportional force
That repels
Yet excitedly attracts
The dimness
Of floating purpose
Gaseous
Now unrefined
In atomic
And splintered majesty
Of a universe
Expanding in hate
The lonely bodies
That wander and seek

A place
To rest before
God
Reveals
His numbers.

We Hung Out (War)

I mourn
The sorrowful plea
Of a friend
Desperate for change
His tired
And inward gaze
Layers beneath his eyes
Violet
Black
And staggered
The cascading folds of his flesh
Concealing
A hidden lava
Combusting
Ready to burst

I'm worried
It's the mark of age
A flag
Of fading years
His chance
To make a difference
Wasted
On futile tasks
Caught
In raging sands
Caving
To jagged earth
Solace
In paper bags
Guns
On wooden desks

Napalm
In his chest
The suicide of nameless conflict
All for greedy drafts
Service
His full-time job
More like
Line of action
All the poverty
And building destruction
The grind can ever deploy

We hung out
Late last night
Of course
We spoke of war.

Taking the Initiative

The deep pockets
And bleeding inkwells
Strewn along
Banks of happenstance
Are the fancy suits
And scattered flowers
Of bouquets
For working corpses
Who initiate
The solemn liturgy
Of money
Orgasms
And death
In the quest
For missing life
Like poetry
A call for help.

Beg for Applause

We judge
The worst achievements
By the best
Of our selfish turns
A cruel and divisive whim
Of a criticism
For the dogs.

Those
Who persist
Regardless
All
Any
Or none…
How do they perform?
By whom
Do they make
Their pay?

Saw a Movie

Let me be as honest
To tell you how I've grown
Unsteady
Unspeakably lost
In lifetimes
Failed from the start

Today
I sat in the theater
Awaiting
A blackened sanctuary
As the grainy and distant image
Made fluid
The yearning motion
Projected from
Deepened memory
Like a reel of tattered cells
I'd imagined
To be a tale of frames
Strewn across
Visible history

But the story
Played out like fiction
We anticipate only in truth
As the hero
Sought cause in a woman
Just to capture
The hope in her death

I'm afraid
It speaks too much
To the frail and beloved memento
I'd stored in my eyes

Of you
Now hidden in the sight
Of minutes
Passing
From the second you left

I'm like
That immortal archetype
Who saves children
From captors and bullies
Adults from themselves and money
Lovers from the comfort of sex

It's the tears
I shed in spite of it
The willingness
To endure
In emptiness
The moment I've stalled
In spitefulness
Perpetually
Like a picture of worth
Cut from a cardboard image
On the bricks
In an alley of mind

Somewhere
Near the ending
I realized
The moral was loneliness
Discontent
With grace everlasting
Never tasting
Or feeling the angel
Only knowing
Her scent is there

Beyond
The tangible meaning
I've sullied
By a measure of sadness
And forgetting
That glistening hour
As the streak of tears
Subsides

We all
Are building
Toward innocence

Some of us
Need pain
Just to see it.

Button Stuck

I don't really
Think
(That deeply or
Admittedly
All that much)
But I know
Which half
Has been
Severed
Or sold
At a lesser value
Rescinded
And all at once
Punished
For being too close
To the words
Or flirting
With the death
Of myself
At the cost of
Remaining sane
Or staying
In the sheath
Of abuse
Rather than
Being that blade
Every other
Expects me
To be

And cutting
For the sake of killing
Or slicing
In the hopes of condemning

A docile
But antagonized
Child
Whose lie
Is the insult of manliness
Or jobs
Or money
Or happiness
Foretold
At the moment of birth
But ended
The second
They think.

We the Aimless

John had
A certain diligence
In the remarkable
Way he chose
To study and maintain
Such efforts
The manner
In which he was shaped
And raised by aging parents
Who remembered
Their booming nation
As it was
Before he grew
When the pride and poetry of usefulness
Was a staunch disclaimer of freedom
But rewarded
With suburbs and dolls
Housewives
Sitters
And playthings
With kitchenettes
Salaries
Securities
Tucked into tinier nests
Humble like
The flattest of whites
Used to paint patios
Or porches
As the neighborhoods
Lay still in the summer
Awnings
Covered days in the sun
And tomorrow
Was a lavish chore

Hurried
But notably savored
Like the moments
Of marital bliss
His mother
Hadn't felt in her heart
But father
Swore he did with another
At a motor inn
In some adjacent state
On the last of his days
To sell
Just before
The commute caught up

How peculiar and appealing
The lie
Shimmered across laminate paper
And stole
What rebellion remained
As it hung
On the office wall
And told of
Beers and dormitories
But no experience
Or worth
Or ideals
To uphold in a post-Towers world
And market made false
By the ruins
Of the greedy and elastic tendrils
By the hands
Of those like his folks
Greasy
Grubby
But ignorant

Wanton in seeking excess
But lying sore with illness
In a home
After funds ran cold
And their kids
Grew numb to warmth
Cause that's
What they learned
From the best

His sister
Joan
Was a girl
Neglected
Ignored
And coddled
Reduced to
A haircut and nails
The colors
Of a cheapened dress
That became
Her entire identity
The day that she realized
She lost
Cause the game
Was rigged from beginning
And the bias
Was her guidance from home

She
Unlike John
Was an image
Whereas he
Was the projection
Of a ghost

Not real
Or actual
Or permissible
But coined
In the wayward mint
Of progress lost to dreams
And history
Unaware of its cost

Equally unequal they are
Joan
John
And the rest

The graduates
High schoolers
Coeds

Brothers
Sisters
And kin

Under thirty
Unemployed and aimless
As they wander
The promise exposed
Long ago unearthed as lies
They remain
Transient as phantoms
Or dreamers
Stifled by hopes
Not breadwinners
But artists unruly
And their breakups
From intangible needs

Begging in the street for conquests
Or the love and sincere acknowledgment
Of a soul
Accepted as valid.

Sudden Turns

Don't you
Inwardly seethe
When people
Try to say:
"You do what
You gotta do—
It's just how
We have to get by"?

Let me
Put it bluntly:
You don't really
Have to do
Anything.

This is all just
Empty space,
And we're lines
In every direction,
Passing
But never meeting,
Like a fixed point
Of human folly
In the matters
Of perpetual black.

Don't settle
For half-assed philosophy
Or accept
The burden of ease—
The complacent
Ties to conformity
And desk job
Or marriage lifelessness.

Be the crossing
Of missing ends;
Realize
God is a wall
(Or a doorway
If you prefer),
And take some
Sudden turns.

Carousel (Richmond Avenue)

Willowbrook (Till Next Time)

We painted that faded canvas at the end of Eton Place.

You and me, two scarred hands sinking in tangled palms as they cupped those wandering fingers that set out on an autumn stroll for that afternoon and into the absent thereafter.

We carved our initials on the trees, forever in bark and fog as the last of the summer flowers wilted from their drained yellows into a hue of melancholy morass—yielding to winter's grasp in the time it took us to be inspired, as the key I used to impress fell to the ground where we kissed.

I willed that etch to last.

In some ways, the phantoms do too.

You said it would be admired by our kids. I believe you now when I see that park.

Shades stalk the trail of our journey. They are specters of a solemn exchange hunting down the footsteps of us: the merry-go-round and our August sanctuary, park benches after lunch and drinks, sitting close to avoid wind chills and loneliness as we talked about potentialities near the lakefront—lifetimes and fairytales spoken in that private kingdom obscured by shrubs.

Allow me the solace in confessing that I'll love you until time gives way—for an ember in these darkened hours that speak to my noblest of attempts. In this, I recall sanctity and courage. In this, I remember bargaining for tomorrow—for a premature heartbeat and silenced verse as I knelt down and worshiped that promise at the edge of God's great fantasy, about love between vagabond souls and the commitment to keep my purpose as yours while the family looked on from the table; and for once everything was right in my world.

It was Thanksgiving, and you cried to me gently, "Of course, I will. Of course."

I found virtue at the end of the universe, where, on the tides of her joyful tears, I saw Christ call out from Calvary the forgiveness of mankind's sins and the covenant of love to one man...an inconsequential, undeserving man... fulfilled by the vow of this girl—impossible, improbable, and wonderful as the existence of a deity in the universe. That same cosmos I sometimes called godless. The same one that remained void of substance...until it brought you into the fold, and religion became the stars on your lips as they tasted of celestial certainty and the promise of piety unseen.

Now, when I drive past that road, there is a still life that tells of its artists— youngsters in the paints of passion with everyone but their impulses to blame.

It will never be a woodland or playground where two people kindled the purest of sins. Rather, it is a time and place housed in a shattered monument that perpetually teeters on the tip of my shortcomings—immortalized in grass and stone, dirt, and muddied water as a tribute to the greatest gift of a life now discontent without her. *Permanently unmatched and swayed by the briefest of aeons with you.*

Engaged until you threw it away...to find another image for your canvas.

I'll never paint again without a muse. I'll always be here waiting for mine.

From a boy who couldn't be a man, wondering why my color left...till next time she never steps out of the car.

Till next time.

Forever Hold Your Peace

This one is for the men who tried too hard—the sour loafers and dynamite moochers who walked in on love with a fiend. Doggy-styled, roughed up, and satisfied by instinct's macho call and display.

It's a prayer built on apathy and vengeance, on sofas and phone calls to loved ones as inadequacy ferments in your heart.

Friends help you stir the elixir.

"Better to be bitter and broken."

"Better to be burnt and bloated."

Better to be flaccid and sexless. They don't say it, but it cracks in their tone.

She never wanted a boy.

That's you; that's the subject to the alpha—her shrine to muscle and mayhem, miscalculated and misjudged by her ethics—merely beckoned and affirmed in her loins.

No, she never wanted a youngster.

Just children she can distort into adults, through her vestige of purpose and heartlessness as the cycle spirals downward until dusk.

And by dark she hears her verse in the forest, resounding in her patriarch's howl—a rugged and booming call of holiness, distanced in abuse and swagger—that father and conqueror of loners, of lowly virgins and impotent geeks.

"Go forth and multiply the foolish, for theirs is the very belief of heaven."

They'll burrow in the mercy of religion if it means vindicating the carnal sins of that cave—their bedroom, their enclosure of sex. Redeemed not even by matrimony, only in the downfall of man through its progeny—its poetry of senselessness and productivity, stacked up like models on a game board, just waiting to be slaves to the dice.

That was never you by her side.

That was never you in her arms.

You were only good for sizing up to that jewel. And a cheap fuck before her bear came home.

Chasing you from those woods. Forever holding your peace.

Never Date a Hippie ('Cause You'll Fall in Love and She Won't Stay)

You said we'd read our children folktales of midnight smiles, blanketing the dusted plains and shimmering with a course of stars—that canvas of missing daylight and the trail of its lingering gaze, illuminating the sacred canyons as our lovemaking shook the wilderness and rumbled the sands of feeling with the plight of dusk near its peak.

From the heights of celestial knowledge came the ringing of wooden chimes, marking the blessed union with the echo of heavenly sound—little guardians and innocent spectators yet to be born of flesh, infants like the ones you promised—iridescence on the tips of their fingers, the breath of nature in their nose. So gentle and indistinguishable from the instinct in your eyes, the evening colors of your face, painted like the fallen horizon as you collapsed on my chest in the bed, and the brush of my inspired soul remained one with your fount of color—gushing acrylics between your legs, leaking oils on the skin of your thighs—that palette bleeding me dry as I begged for one last stroke to make sure our picture was conceived in art through the bliss of God.

It was never brought to fruition—you lied about the path of angels in the wake of that setting sun.

All that stands is your portrait, lost to these basement walls, suited to its musty stillness, those streaks of hair in my sheets, smeared with the stains of abandonment...torn along the seams in agony—the only memory I have left of you: a vision of rainbows on her dress and free-spirited afternoons, talking communes and the fall of capitalism as you tasted sex in her speech. Philosophy on her tongue, flowers along her bosom, psychedelics in her gut— *electric candy daydreams glowing neon on the soles of her feet.*

A relic of our forgotten desert and the tribe you promised in love.

Sitting Room

I am not a winner.

Just deadpan
Swallowed
Untold.

Reflective of my ills
Superior to a point
Extended in their reach
Dangling an amateur rope
In the downplay
Of coming flames
Words to a burning edge
Severing the knotted brink
Insipid
Lyrically inane.

I welcome the turn of ages.

I spin the seasons of phrase.

What majesty
Hallowed grief
To narrate a prism alone
Crystallize the passing spectrum
Distill a color of wavelengths
The threshold of teetering sense
Washed in a course of sound
So ugly
Aghast
Yet swollen
Throbbing in fearful pride
Painful
Rested and known

Expected
Like midday turns
In the dust between hated walls
Settling now as gray
Entering through its beam
Wandering a settled silence
And praying for broken noise
A poem in focused light:

The pretense of being certain
Knowing deaf ears are the jealous type.

Note on Table

Regardless
Of rampant ills
Despite
Your cunning flaws
I would die
Each wasted second
Of glowing days spent in those arms
Come fortune
Or material ruin
Silence
Or rained salvation
Like prayers on the palms of hands
Grace in the sweat of days
Hours in the folds of cheeks
What I'd do
To take back those sins
Covered
In fountains of smiles
Tangled
In weeds and friends

I could pretend
To be a man.

You Told Me to Watch the Moon

I miss
The waxing crescent
Of "I love you"
In the night
And fear
The hollow crater
Of coarseness
In my bed
The empty and fragrant
Indent
Of a shadow
Cold and dim
Once
An outline of souls
Now a half
Of jagged ends
A waltz
In the breath of ink
Captive
In blackened skies
Swollen
Gray
And sacred
The mark
Of a moonlit coupling
Radiance unabashed
So particular
In its madness
The universe
Speaking hymns
To romance
Under stars.

The Dance after the Ceremony (Nine O'Clock Sharp)

This awkward stance
Of dagger eyes
Trusted scars
And memories in repose
Await the vow of moonlight
Like nocturnes in ballroom halls
Weddings of shadowed abbeys
Ballads on the tips of fingers
Slender
Graceful
Poised
Like the rush of blood to wounds
Festered on lovers' hands
And memories hidden in cellars
Contemplating bottled potential
Aged now
But wasted
Like wine.

The Glass Cabinet

From where I tread
It watches
Glares
In glimmering distance
Shimmers
On fractured ends
Glittering
Like angled stars
Mirrors of failing suns
Refracted in narrow space
Starlight
And dazzling hope
Cut on edge by diamond
To bridge
The stretch of lifetimes
Bound to thriving systems
Orbiting
Within her ring
Now returned to primary ether
Its shelf so lifelessly drawn
A universe of forgotten potential
As I pass through
The jewelry aisle
To exit through despair
And coats.

Misaligned

Counting all putrid instants
That twist and perturb my thoughts
And gnaw at the smallest glow
Snarl at beloved dusk
To itch or eat its poisons
And drink from the brackish well
To binge, unsettled, on instincts
Knotted and fetid ribbons
Insides captured and spit
Emptier
Vapid
And splendid
Respite for a granted wish
The tear of inhuman husks
All worth the sight at the well
Copper and dreadful tolls
Where pennies and nightmares dwell.

Happy Toys

Mother
I never wanted
To die
In the ways I have
Or trace
The petrified boardwalks
Of studded
And unsteady youth
Where smiles
Are wooden hours
Stoic and stifled radiance
Like sunshine
On porcelain figures
Painted
With rosy cheeks
But marred
By years of use
Bruised and beaten by cowards
Whose glue
Was a foreign hand
And knife an empty shelf
To cry as I have
For stability
To beg as I have
For innocence
And plead with girls
For forgiveness
Even though
I'd done nothing wrong
But remember
The sadder days
Of treading
That lighted pathway
With the same

And imagined stare
Of characters
Stories
And images
Like chiseled
And lonely puppets
Looking
For a string of peace.

Male Gaze

Maybe he had it
All wrong
How the music
Of a woman's affection
Wasn't chocolate
Grace
Or ambition
Or the confidence
To steal her soul
But the fortitude
To acknowledge reflections
In the strength
Of her straining image
Acceptance
Of wary hearts
And the sour
Judgmental gaze
Of glass
Looking back from the wall
As it told her
Of fleeting empowerment
When the universe
Remained
In her womb
And the mirror
Was a tragic conduit
Of all the ungodly terms
And avatar
Of damaging words
Marring her
Mounting divinity
In the soul and form
Of ecstasy
Taken flesh

As a child of God
Far from
A bouquet of flowers
Or the image made false
On a screen.

Postmanic Pixie Syndrome

It's as relevant as the shallowness
In the outward curve of her heels
And the pointed purple boots
Running with tears and fetishes
His idea of a perfect girl
Or a fantasy cut from rejects
Or an object to emulate angels
In the soft and vinyl crackle
Of a warmth that pops like grooves
As we age and forget she's human
Not a character
Reel
Or canvas
Made to withhold a sketch
But instead breathe life from stars
Under awnings and Tuesday rains
As she waddles in from the image
And makes the room her painting
A collection of visionary stares
With the city a backdrop behind her
And the palette a sound of weather
Gentle on dripping glass
As she adjusts a fiery hat
And tassels her auburn ringlets
And plays with the reddest beret
While acknowledging the shine on her cheeks
Like a polish of palest light
As she calls
Eludes
And echoes
All the deepest and altogether flawed
Needs of an inexperienced heart
By the way she dawdles and breathes
And takes in the thickness of melancholy

Unfurled from her billowing dress
Through the wry and ensnaring smile
Which speaks to all her divinities
The priestess and traveler of quirkiness
The showoff
Mendicant
And scholar
Thus men would make her seem
Through fear and foreignness of intellect
Exhibited by the browsing poetess
Goddess of laptops and piercings
Sitting in his most sacred of sections
All alone and reading philosophy
Waiting for the bedroom kisses
And caressing the sheets of happenstance
To insist on commingling flesh
As a union of wayward opposites
In the second he realizes she's gone
And impossible like the movies had told him
She'd be as a dream made true.

Last Time I Need Something to Sleep

I'm admitting
I'm a lonely person
And the problem
Is in the partners
The women
Crushes
And wanderers
Who swear by
The swoon of attachment
But deceive
By that ambiguous word
Struggling
To gain a conscience
As gray as
The will of their hands
And elusive
In a stammering kiss
That marks
Like a scarlet scowl
Of affections bright and made
Fabricated
Like sequined rags
But delicate
To the passer's touch
As they tell you
To be more sociable
Even as social
As you've become
Or to fear
The wary sickness
Of missing
Their frequent gaze
As they miss
Their daily visit

Or meander
To dangle a stick
Of carrots
Like attractive flesh
Just waiting to be enjoyed
Or nourished
By the need of a beau
But not
The one she is with
Who has changed
A thousand faces
And scoured
A vacant multiverse
Of possibilities
Where she never stayed
But blamed
The wanton solitude
Of a writer
Who baked his soul
At the core
Of a swelling sun
And throbbed
To the beat of her pulse
As she carried him
From death to life
To death and life
And back again
Round
And round
The constellations
As she coveted and begged
For a God
In the streak
Of rainbow affections
In the arms
Of a common Adonis

And not the neurotic
And beautiful
Aurora
Of a spitfire man whose grace
Is anything but perfection
Whose hell
Is a written word
Yet conviction
Is a golden proof
Of the virtue
Awaiting his brokenness
To seek
Greater stars in the distance
Without
The hand of a girl
Or oppressive
Illusion of sex
As the story of us
Would relay
As I remain
On the carpet to sleep
With the television
A source of comfort
And an herbal pill
In my clasp.

Boarded Up

So much
Can be said
Of a nail
How it shreds
Through a plank
Like bone
And tethers its fate
To a wall
With bits and screws
Of framework
That hold
A lifetime in place
But not until
It leaves its scars
Or mutilates
An appearance of worth

How it chips
And erodes
Over decades
Is deemed
Uninhabitable
By cause
And mauls
The faith of pillars
Before falling
On those who built
Like a man
Forgiven at Calvary
Or a criminal
Absolved of wrongs

How typical
Of aging real estate

To be stripped
By a crew
In seconds
If the wood
Has lost its semblance
And is petrified
By accusing halls
Empty
And hopelessly echoed
A cavernous and ringing void
Now home
To ghosts unstable
Yielding
As an enduring structure
But felt
Like an accepted memory

I thought
When I passed
The corner
Where they had it
Boarded up
That sometimes
We value one change
For materials
Of a second lease
Like the drugstore
Where I'd take you
Now a sign
For another sale.

Sharrotts Road

WRECK OF PROSE

As salt is the burden of oceans, so is this need to be read.

The time I waste on approval is sunk like a boat lost to the brine—a test of the furious Atlantic consumed and marked by its depths. Semantics swallowing hulls, phrases ravaged on starboard. Bows poised in angles—downward, flooded, and empty.

I dream underwater in shipwrecks. I sleep with fishes and figments.

And within the widening abyss, I lift layers of pressurized ego as mermaids seduce the muse and lead her to bigger yachts—brighter islands and bluer waters where others just float with prose. Gifted and peeling at fruits—savoring the sugary sweet nectar, reveling in tropical gifts.

Why must I bear the barnacles of verbs consumed in disaster—grotesque maritime wonders forsaken in passing age?

Binging, aching, fearing. Composing, clicking, clacking. Instigating, intimidating, aggravating. Wandering, neglecting, nurturing. Attempting, failing, winning. Losing, loving, dying. Revising, reading, and writing.

Writing. *Fucking writing. All of the above and then some.*

God hated me, so he gave me words.

Now I'm waiting for someone to listen.

But everyone else *is* listening…

Listening to everyone…

But me.

To Live, Love, and Die in Suburbia

In the ravine behind my eyes
I circle
Midnight lots
Scour
Crumbling asphalt
Park near
Neighborhood haunts
Kneel at
Fallen monuments
And crank the hymns of strip malls
In stereos
Accumulated deafness
The wear and tear of youths
Juveniles
Forlorn miscreants
Arcade heroes
Skateboard myths
Under the fluorescent dimness
The stare of gas station lights

How I miss the reckless pit stops
Delis
After-hour calls
Pharmacies and diner breakfasts
As early as the birthing sun
Stalled in front of your house
Kissing
In silent cars
Always
Our devoted ritual
Always
Our scripted Mass

I ask God every night
To save that sliver of peace
The beautiful hell in my dreams
Make it my personal heaven
When I leave
This grayscale afterthought
For now
A stable absence.

Category Unknown

This tempest in my gut
Speaks of scathing winds
Coarse sands
And troubled rains
That reside in vacant drawers
On the desk
Where I kept your image
Framed
Like hanging clouds
Silver
Suspiciously still
Now vacuous as a storm
At the center of my world
Where the eye
Is its deepest
Hell.

Lighthouse

Must I
Carry these features
Of vanity
Insolence
And grace
To the coast
Where prisoners linger
And argue their cage
With the ocean
An indemnity of possible choice
The freedom to reclaim these shores
And at once
Be given a chance
At finding
Their guiding beacon
While the boat of sin
Still sinks
And carries their misfortune
On tides
To the deepest and most muddled
Of seas
Where wreckage and forgiveness
Lay flat
On the silence
Of altars submerged
To God
To forsaken cathedrals
This religion of salted tears
And the discontent of manic waves
A remnant
Like sacrificed hours
As the penance
Of a lonely brine.

Tide

Every distance
Every ocean
Is a promise
Kept to you:
Timeless
Forever fluid
Endless…
With the waves.

Behind a Good Man

Any man can lead.
It takes a faithful one
To grow
And a woman to see the change,
How her love becomes the flame
And sparks the raging catalyst
To burn
At the core of his soul—
A religion
Of heartened virtue
Only she
Has the power to wield.

Why It Hurts

Hate
Is an approach
Toward empathy
Painted
With streaks
Of reflection.

Gallery

It is good to be sad this day,
To cry a tear of oils,
And bleed a show of paints,
To make the blessed sacrifice,
In curves and captured moments,
Oils stroked like hair,
Canvas tenderly caressed,
Colors sweat in passion,
Sexing the heated muse,
As she bears her flesh in mystery,
Fostering a sacred impulse,
Collective and unrestrained,
Of madmen and poets with pens,
Prophets and sages with palettes,
And lunatic saints with brushes,
Their sordid tryst a prayer,
Between the legs of a goddess,
Fulfilled in golden frames,
And immortalized once in sin,
Flaws so unbearably human,
It revokes the sanctity of God,
Makes him startlingly real,
Converts his majesty to skin,
And reduces heaven to now,
In the unity of man's potential,
As God becomes a line…
Traced by one of us.

Blossomed Muse

Tell me
How unoriginal
Anguish and tattered edges
Essence on empty pages
Insomnia in ink
Paper rendered speechless
Piled from tortured attempts
Crumbled sheets of triumph
People caught dead in text
Are reason enough
For judgment
Venom smeared like oil
Vinegar a hateful stench
Wafting from the drip
Of fluids distilled in rage
Elixir of jealous contempt
Savored, swallowed, imposed
By those who verse with cinders
Rather than bear their gospel
In blood
In love
In sentences
Bouquets of a blessed phrase
Flowers on a spoken throne
Verbal and linguistic majesty
Deserved
Of praise and holiness
Coined
From sacred truth
Not thorns
Of talentless weeds
Sapping vision
From dying roots

Drying
The blossomed muse
Sequenced
In colorless order.

Frayed Nerve

I think I'll dig a dream
And bury my faith below
Sleeping in shadowed hopes
Praying on shattered glass
Blanketed by ashen grace
Obscured on blood and knees
This time and tirade of lunatics
To savor the loss of feeling
And value the gamble of rosaries
Singed by holy flame
Swollen like painful saints
And vindicated in the lack of touch
Of her
By women
Or purpose
This disconnect
This severed line
To what makes
Sensation
Spark.

Priorities (Make Them Right)

Never deal in numbers
Or little green paper fucks
Who dictate souls
Like property
Or fluctuate
With government standards.

Instead
Smell the air of value
In each breath
Of human worth
And see
The image of godliness
In the smile of
Loving mothers
Fathers
Families
And the sick
The laughter of imagining children
The blessing of a couple's embrace
Or church of the inspired artist
A saint of the sacred muse
Who needs
The touch of her embers
For the cinders
To kindle her heart
And like Christ
Build a level of sacrifice
Committed to flesh and blood
To easels

Inks
And melody
To feeling
Emphasis
And love.

Leaps of Faith

This distinct
And valued testament
Is a covenant
Of raging color
A blitz of
Empty promises
My rainbow
Of dripping words
Like the pleasure
Of needy faithful
And the touch
Of maddened apostles
Stomping the sacred vow
In vengeance against the law.

Allow me
To acquire justice
In the tongues
Of forgotten vagrants
The chords
Of suicide halos
And abandon
Of callous saints
Who found the path to heaven
In the bottle
Of an empty pill
The brim
Of a seething liquor
And ecstasy
Of a Midas touch
Where everything
Turned to rage
And the leap of faith
Was a feast

For rummaging
In wasted time
And dabbling
In the flow of impulse
Christ
Eros
Thanatos
Sharing tables
With a miscreant muse
And the fuck of a virgin feeling
Birthed in the lies of men.

Father Capodanno

The building stank of numbness
In the agony of its crumbling facade
Walls without purpose or ends
And bricks with powdery substance
Chiseled like a mark of distinction
History in the billowing clouds
Of dirt from the fumes and fixtures
That cracked like a wrinkling face
And peered into immediate death
From the way the air settled so blankly
And lingered as heavy as agedness.

Down the boulevard they went
Oblivious and understated
Pedestrians who made their curse
And bystanders hating the traffic
But accepting the end of the world
Served to them on college degrees
Or vindicated in certified paychecks
From a company that traded in testaments.

This city is a living effigy
And altogether a nauseous collection
Of entitlement
Bureaucracy
And hardship
Of the concern for paperwork meaning.

A collection of indefinite tombs
That line the gum-coated streets
Near its passing
Near the crossroads
Of tragedy under offerings
Of billboards to delude the proud

Who recall the name so vaguely
But selectively neglect the circumstance.

I can't and it makes me sick
To know how nothing has changed
Indelibly
And perhaps
So purposefully
'Cause very little will make us repent
Or content enough to remember
As they carry on with their jobs
Return to the shops they had sold
But forever suppress that evening
When we realized
Impermanence was home.

I (Fear) New York

Early this weekend morning
At a corner
Near Lexington Avenue
Stood a raggedy and disheveled woman
With a sign
Across her lap.

It said
In uncouth script
On cardboard in permanent marker
"Homeless in need of food
Please help
I am truly suffering."

A lady
In designer leggings
Trotting to the click of her heels
Said
"Then get a job"
As she stepped into
A limo.

The rest of the passersby
Pretended
She didn't exist
Staring at their glowing phones
Preoccupied with tourist sights
Or thinking of another restaurant
Where they could find lunch
For the day.

None of them
Cared in the slightest

It was evident
In the way they walked
And crossed the street in entitlement
Darting between cars and thoroughfares
Or flipping off aggressive drivers
Without ever stopping to ponder
The female as young as myself
In tatters as she pleaded for lies
In the irony of privileged filth
On the back
Of urban ignorance.

I can't bear
To imagine
Why she should even attempt
Or grow motivated at all
When society treats her so
And mocks the cross of another
When they are the truer Romans
And she the neglected saint
In waiting
For the coming end.

It's why I laugh at peers
Who tell me the city is "exhilarating"
For fun or an evening visit
When sin litters cleaving asphalt
As readily as inhospitality
Or the glares of disinterested strangers
So close and grazing your flesh
But content
Just to stroll in contempt
As they pass
In a fleeting misery
While the crosswalk blinks
For a turn.

It is the most
Unnatural place
Opposed to the human spirit
And breeding of hate or misfortune
Through denial in absurd proximity
And class wars
In broken politics.

I'd rather
Stick to the suburbs
Where the truth
Is plainly obscured
And not deceptively contrived
Where at least we have room to breathe
Where at least there is hope
In solitude.

I pray
That begging woman
Finds God
At the end of her plight
And inherits
More than her slavers
Wallowing in that splendor of stone
And not
The heart of creation
Or tears of a Lord who caved
When he saw
What hell he had made
From creatures who worship glass
As breakable
As it is beautiful
'Cause decadence
Doesn't last in disorder
And permanence
Is easily cracked.

Prime Mover

It's true
What they say of emotion
How it trickles
Like a dew into weeds
And isolates
Its glimmer from sunshine
In the risen
And birthing daylight
From the famed
And unseen ink
To the precious
And circular glow
Of a dim
And paling dark
Where the mirror
Is a dance on water
And the ripple
A symbol of time
Which reaches
Like fingers from man
To the clasp
Of resting creatures
Who are one
In the dirge of creation
And a sound
In the chirping evening
Where mystery
And divinity dwell
At once
Seeking waking radiance
All from
The cascading prism
That echoes
Like geometry of God

And reverberates
Across shapes of perfection
In the flaws
Of revealing sins
Or the moment
Reason became Earth
And made us
Forget that feeling
That brought us
To color and custom
All before
Cultures had clashed.

Blockbuster

I remember
When I was a kid
How the summers used to settle
And remind me of battling dragons
Or knights at the cusp of dawn
Straddling a smoking horizon
As they courted a raving blonde
Elegant
So effervescent
Hair and fallout flowing
Over skylines ruled and maimed
By monsters fighting invaders
Or robots with human feelings
As the cinema lights grew dim
And credits started to roll

I grabbed
My mother's hand
And watched the other kids
The lonely ones
The only children
Smile up at their folks
Who calmed them with a kiss
On the forehead as they sat
Anticipating the screen
As if their gift of life

I particularly remember
The ones born into struggle
Who seemed so perpetually happy
As if the story was just for them
And the hero was their own
A substitute for their pain

And a triumph over hardship
In sixteen-millimeter daydreams
That were a source of personal strength
Like light from a silver sun

I felt for them just as much
And believed that they were legends
In the making of a coming epic
Knowing films could change the soul
And fairytales unite the earth
Like bards in the hands of God

How far has it come?
As I sit here
Half a man
Boy in older shoes
And watch these same theatrics
Believing in this cause
Missing the brighter Mondays
And sunshine afternoons
Where Mom would get me dinner
And buy me a little figure
From the film we had just watched
And promise I was special
Just like those
Ailing peers
As the asphalt grew so heated
It burned to the deepest center
At the core of my swelling need
To create
And speak to this feeling
Where it burst like the August sky
And rained cinders of fiery truth
And comforted the rest
In warmth like fractured stars

I want to believe
Those days

At times
They ring truer still

Looking back
And mourning that purity
Where Mom was always enough
And characters taught us morals
And each toy was a fantastic journey
An opportunity from another world
Escape from the humdrum delirium
Of monotony or responsibility
Certainty
And death

It's true
That's all I want
Still for her to hold me close
And protect me from evil feats
Of business
Money
And illness
To be a light for the voiceless nothings
And maintain that loving innocence
Far from cheating girls
Or the promise of brighter tomorrows
In suits
Or ties
Or marriages
And the delusion of manufactured hopes

For now
I have these blockbusters
I watch those special youths

And feel compelled to be honest
To write
In spite of fury
Against the odds of harsh statistics
And combat the mounting trends
Of a world with no faith in art
Even the most derivative of kinds
Where it still offers truth to the suffering
And enlightens
A big part of the rest.

Twin Lights

I ascend
The unsteady spiral
In haste
To reach its peak
And vacate
A floor of phantoms
As I emulate
A past of storms
And erode
A flag withstanding
The tatters
Of ravenous floods
The glare
Of jealous bricks
In the flash
And shimmering grace
Of whitecaps
On jagged surf
At the summit
Of a teetering knoll
Where the wooden shed
Still stands
And the Queen Anne's lace
Grows thickest
As it faces
The cresting tide
And braces
The Atlantic's breath
As the rusted sand
Still tells
Of the finest
Shipwrecked china
Depicting
An age of glass
From a time

Of porcelain manners
And eloquence
Poised historically
With the image
In royal indigos
Cut
On elephant whites
And the shimmer
Of fragile relics
Fallen
From cargo below
That speaks
Of time overseas
And the voyage
Back home
In sentiment
Toward colonies
Contrarians
And antiquities
Where the remainder
Of goodwill
Still stands
Against the here
And now
Of us
As eavesdroppers
On private pasts

Like trespassers
Walking the decks
Eyeing its mist
From the gates
Treading the grounds of ghosts

Cutting the air
With language
As we peered
From the top
Toward gardens
Locking fingers
In convincing truth
Thinking of men
Who made it
Mourning the ones
Who drowned
And hearing
An echo of franticness
In the guidance
Of wavering beacons
Whose light
Was bridged through distance
But never
Brought close in saving
And the rescue
Was pointless endangerment
As we remember
The Sunday we stood
And felt the unease of sailors
Ferrymen
Keepers
And captains
Maintaining the fire alone
Keeping the oil burning
Providing a star to the missing
Through a glimpse
Of love at the tip
Before kissing
And heading back down.

Run (As Far As You Can)

For you I want studded veils
And lilacs arranged on linens
Women in sequined gowns
Men who can hold their liquor
Beaus who cherish the moment
And value potential for growth
A husband who kneels at your thighs
And gives you a ring each night
In the way he savors your skin
And bundles your soul with touch
A father who willingly pleases
His bride by working as hard
And giving up childish passions
To make them a gift for his kids
As the Bible says he must
As he kisses the infants' feet
And wiggles their curling toes
As you recline there coy and glowing
On sheets in weekend laziness
And he worships the bump on your stomach
And feels the graze of your breath
Savors the willing grace
To be an honest adult
The blessing of a gifted life
Cycle and staunch tradition
Provided and somehow necessary
For all those better than me
More equipped to accept what's passed.

You deserve to run as far
From this as you possibly can
From an obsession with toys and oddities
Novelties, immaturity, and words
His ideal of bliss in solitude
His God of rage and loneliness

In the sinking ink of his pen
The drowning seas of his needs
And the myriad of deaths in his eyes
That pull him from the need to function
And compel his addiction to tears
To glorify the neurotic deceased
And worship the freedom of ills
In the split from accepted lies
And perceive his muse as a sadness
That cannot be quelled with warmth
But only revered in unrest
Sanctified in discontent
And summarized with inflicted harm
Toward himself and his worthless undoing
He's become in trying otherwise
To be anything he could for you

No, I think you should run
Because the circumstance
Still wills it so.

Dumb Philosopher

I confess
To the sleep of the desperate
But indulge
In the barefoot procession
Of arguments
Unleashed in moccasins
And the veil
Of bathrobe conjecture
All before
Coffee has brewed
Or sun
Licks the ear
Of its dreamer
Now awoken
In a stream of radiance
With choice
To erase his illusions
But instead
Breaks even with nerves
Even night
Couldn't hope to relieve
But instead
Makes sense through a thought
Too crazy
Too abstract
To behold.

Carried (from Water)

There used to be a bench
Where the shoreline met the waves
At the foot of climbing grass
Near the edge of brackish swells
That rippled with golden rocks
Like a ridge of coastal pockets
With fish the size of pennies
And flowers close to land
Reds and sun-kissed saffron
In a garden just offshore

My father used to sit there
And savor the sea-soaked breeze
As the wind kissed his salty cheeks
And reminded him of legends
Told to him as a child
And passed on through his words
Like a text of recent gospel
Like a fable unveiled in storms

He spoke of how jealous oceans
Claimed precious lives each day
In exchange for tides and volume
Striking fear in the heart of man

God had made this pact
In an effort to appease the depths
And offer a false security
To men and wayward sailors
As fishers who use its bounty
For profit outside of nature

It was through this secret testament
That the promise emerged as truth

And shipwrecks plagued the currents
And drowning was a dangerous genesis
Rebirth at the hands of forces
Divine and equal to heaven
Like Christ with John the Baptist
Who knelt at the pool in reverence
Of his father's just decision
To cleanse and take in instants
With the fury of a singular means
Engulfed in staunch conviction

Now that bench is gone
After October spelled its end
November took its toll
And the island saw its season

For I choose to see such loss
As acceptance of a new approach
And ability to start once more
To walk in the paths of holiness
By entitling collective efforts
In the pursuit of common needs
And establish a branch of sacredness
That extends beyond land or surf
In the wake of flooded losses
And triumph of damaged neighbors
Acknowledging a sturdier pier
Built with better intentions
After taken in swift calamity
And lined with harsher truths

Acknowledgments

This collection would have remained an unfulfilled ambition (and nearly possible dream) without the assistance, tutelage, and love of the most important people in my life. All of the following individuals remain instrumental in my devotion to the art of writing. They propel me toward the stars and all at once ground me in their orbit. They are believers above and beyond—a choir of devoted confidants and mentors who keep me whole. I couldn't live without them. They bear witness to these words in every possible sense:

- My mother and father, Linda and Dominick Pigno, for having the courage to inspire and raise a child who wasn't afraid to question. They nourished what was different and fed my need for expression—to foster the pursuit of knowledge through learning to love oneself. To them, I owe my life. They are, forever, my world.
- My overwhelming gratitude and affection for Amanda Rollizo, who helped me compile these pieces and stood by me in the darkest hours. She is the woman who gave me the chance and the grace to accept the present—with eyes toward a better future and belief, once more, in happiness.
- Dr. Rita Reynolds—an incredible teacher and role model. Her guidance has been utterly priceless. Her friendship is worth even more. Thank you for knowing I can (even when I thought I couldn't). Thank you for always listening and remaining a part of my life—long after class was over and college was a distant memory.
- To my friends throughout the years, from Farrell up through Wagner—for lending their support and providing an open ear. I consider you each a brother. You all know who you are.
- And for anyone I might have missed—family and other heroes, from the known to the slightly obscure. There are far too many to list. But in my heart, you are never far away.

About the Author

Jonathan Pigno is a writer from Staten Island, New York. He is an alumnus of Wagner College and Monsignor Farrell High School. His work has been featured in numerous publications, including *Vine Leaves Literary Journal, Asbury Pulp, Five 2 One Magazine,* and *365 Tomorrows*. Additionally, Jon's prose has been showcased in local periodicals such as *SI View, Taste Magazine,* and *The Staten Island Advance.*

When he is not writing, Jon loves to waste his time in front of countless movies, comic books, video games, and other forms of literary or pop-culture media on a daily basis. He currently resides at home with his family and beloved Maltese, Gabby.

www.ingramcontent.com/pod-product-compliance
Lightning Source LLC
LaVergne TN
LVHW041259080426
835510LV00009B/798